This book is presented to:

_____

By:

_____

On:

_____

God, I Need to Talk to You

STORIES ABOUT GOD'S LOVE AND FORGIVENESS

Dan Carr
and
Susan K. Leigh

Pictures
by Bartholomew
and
Bill Clark

CONCORDIA PUBLISHING HOUSE • SAINT LOUIS

Published 2018 by Concordia Publishing House
3558 S. Jefferson Avenue, St. Louis, MO 63118-3968
1-800-325-3040 · cph.org

Written by Dan Carr and Susan K. Leigh.

Text copyright © 1984, 2005, 2011, 2012 Concordia Publishing House

Illustrations copyright © Concordia Publishing House

Scripture quotations are from the ESV® Bible (The Holy Bible, English Standard Version®), copyright © 2001 by Crossway, a publishing ministry of Good News Publishers. Used by permission. All rights reserved.

Manufactured in Shenzhen, China/022100/300683

1 2 3 4 5 6 7 8 9 10   26 25 24 23 22 21 20 19 18 17

To all God's forgiven and redeemed children.
Pray without ceasing. 1 Thessalonians 5:17

TABLE OF CONTENTS

Do not be anxious about anything,
but in everything by prayer and supplication
with thanksgiving let your requests
be made known to God.
Philippians 4:6

Dear Parent:

God calls you to parenthood, and along with that comes the privilege and responsibility of teaching your child about life as a Christian. You begin when he is very young by folding his little hands while you pray during the worship service and at bedtime. You expand on that by teaching mealtime prayers and the Lord's Prayer. Your child quickly learns to imitate your actions.

At first, such prayers are extensions of verbal development, like reciting the ABCs and saying "please" and "thank you." But somewhere around the age of three, your child will begin to understand that he is praying to Someone. And by the time he has started school and is increasingly exposed to the world and other people, his comprehension of sinful behavior and the need for forgiveness expands.

Along with the model of prayer you establish in church at and home, you can use this book to help your child learn that

- God hears all prayers in Jesus' name;
- He is faithful to answer them in accordance to His will for us; and
- no prayer is too big or too little; we can pray about anything at any time.

May this book, along with other prayer books in your home, be a touchpoint as you guide and nurture your child's spiritual formation.

The authors

God, I Need to Talk to You about BAD MANNERS

Written by Susan K. Leigh
Pictures by Bill Clark

CONCORDIA PUBLISHING HOUSE · SAINT LOUIS

I know all about "please" and "thank you."
I **always** say those words, so I thought I had
good manners. But now, Lord, I know about
other manners, too. **Bad ones.**

I learned that **interrupting** the teacher is bad manners.

Mrs. Johnson sure didn't like it when I interrupted in class today. I was excited when I knew the answer and I wanted to say it first. I raised my hand. I waved my arm. And I shouted the answer before she called on me.

The race is not to the swift.
Ecclesiastes 9:11

13

I learned that not saying thank you for a gift is bad manners and is wrong.

Mom's friend brought me a birthday gift. When she asked how I liked it, I shrugged my shoulders and rolled my eyes. I didn't like it at all. Besides, my birthday was last month.

I learned that slurping my milk at the dinner table is bad manners. Actually— slurping my milk **anywhere** is bad manners.

Patience is better than pride. Ecclesiastes 7:8

17

And, God, I learned that interrupting
Dad when he's on the phone is bad manners.
I wanted to talk to Grandma, too.
But Dad said I shouldn't have yelled.
I should have waited patiently and quietly
until it was my turn to talk.

After I talked to Grandma, Dad told me that good manners are important all the time. Good manners mean I care about other people and I want to be kind and considerate to them. Good manners mean I show **Jesus' love** for me by the way I behave toward others.

As dearly loved children ...
live a life of love, just as Christ
loved us. Ephesians 5:1-2

God, I don't mean to be rude. Dad told me he would help me learn better manners. Mom said she would get a book about manners from the library so we can read it together.

I told them both I was sorry and I would try to be patient and kind and wait my turn.

Now that I know about good manners, God, I want to say "thank You" for sending Your Son, Jesus, who died for my sins. I know You forgive me. And "please," God, help me remember my manners every day. **Amen.**

God, I Need to Talk to You about MY BAD TEMPER

Written by Dan Carr

Pictures by Bartholomew and Bill Clark

CONCORDIA PUBLISHING HOUSE · SAINT LOUIS

Dear God,

I am talking to You from my room.
I am being punished by Mom and Dad.
I need Your help, God, because
I have a very ...

bad temper.

When I got up this morning, I could not
find one of my shoes. I was angry because I
was scared Mom would be angry at me for
losing it. So I **punched** my little brother.
I thought he had hidden my shoe on purpose.

A quick-tempered man
does foolish things.
Proverbs 14:17

Then, for breakfast,
Mom made oatmeal.
She knows **I hate oatmeal.**
She never makes what I like.
So I **shoved** the bowl away
and spilled the milk.

Later, I could not find my bucket
that I use to lift things into my tree house.
So I **punched** my little brother again.
He smiles when Mom says that I am not
careful. I hate it when Mom thinks
that my brother is better than I am.

When I am afraid, I will trust in You.

Psalm 56:3

When Dad came home,
he would not take me fishing
as he had promised. **I slammed the door.**
That is when Mom and Dad
took me to my bedroom.

We talked about what happened.

My shoe was in my closet,
where I had thrown it.

My bucket was in the garage,
where I had filled it with things
to take to the tree house.

And Dad wanted to go fishing,
but he had a meeting.

Then Mom and Dad said, "We know you want to be nicer, but sometimes you are so afraid that you get angry."

They told me that I **never** have to be afraid that they don't love me or that You, God, don't love me.

Whoever comes to Me
I will never drive away.
John 6:37

So, here I am, Jesus.
I am really sorry for what I did.
    Teach me to remember that
my family really does **love me**
and **forgives me,** just as **You do.**
    Help me show others
how much **love** I have,
especially my little brother. Amen.

God, I Need to Talk to You about BAD WORDS

Written by Susan K. Leigh
Pictures by Bill Clark

CONCORDIA PUBLISHING HOUSE • SAINT LOUIS

Mom says I need to **watch my tongue.**

Yesterday, I was frustrated and **I said a bad word.** I knew it was wrong to say it but it just came out.

44

A chattering fool comes to ruin. Proverbs 10:8

You see, it had been a bad day. First my bike had a flat tire. Then I lost my math homework. Then Hannah didn't want to play with me. And then I stubbed my toe on the stairs. **So I said it.**

I thought that if I said something bad, I would feel better. But I didn't—**I felt even worse.**

Words from a wise man's mouth are gracious, but a fool is consumed by his own lips. Ecclesiastes 10:12

I felt **really** bad when I found out
Mom had heard me.

51

Mom explained to me that words like that are **disrespectful and sinful.** When I said it, I dishonored You.

Now I'm **in big trouble** and I can't watch TV for a week. But the worst part is that I shamed myself and I shamed You.

Let your conversation be
always full of grace. Colossians 4:6

Dear Jesus,

You taught me how to show God's love in what I say and what I do. What I said was wrong and I'm sorry. **Forgive me.** (I won't do it again.)

Help me use my words to show everyone how much **You love us and forgive us.** Amen.

God, I Need to Talk to You about BEDTIME

Written by Susan K. Leigh
Pictures by Bill Clark

CONCORDIA PUBLISHING HOUSE • SAINT LOUIS

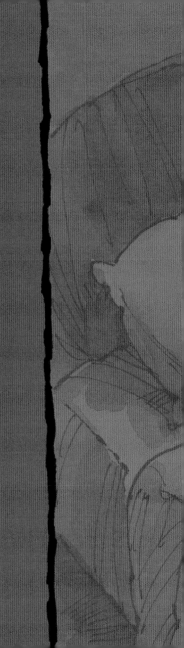

Dear God,

I'm supposed to be getting **ready for bed**. I brushed my teeth. I turned down my covers. And Dad read my favorite book to me. Twice.

Dad kissed me goodnight, and Mom tucked me in. They said my prayers with me. Mom let me have one more drink of water. But I'm **not sleepy!**

Better is a handful of quietness than two hands full of toil and a striving after wind.

Ecclesiastes 4:6

I'd rather watch a movie or play a game. I'd rather read another book or play with my toys.

I **don't** want to go to bed yet.

But Mom and Dad said it's my **bedtime**. They said if I don't get enough sleep, I'll be cranky.

Mom said **everybody** needs to sleep. Grown-ups get to stay up longer, but they still have a regular bedtime. Kids need more sleep because we're growing all the time and that takes a lot of energy.

When you lie down, your sleep will be sweet.

Proverbs 3:24

Dad said that You made day and night so we would have time to work and **time to rest**. We need to rest so we can be strong and healthy. Not cranky.

Then Dad said that even **You rested**. I hadn't thought of that before.

God rested from all His work that He had done in creation.

Genesis 2:3

Mom said **Jesus rested** too. Like the time He was in the boat on the sea and woke up so He could calm the storm.

He awoke and rebuked the wind and the raging waves, and they ceased, and there was a calm.

Luke 14:22

71

So, God, now I understand about getting rest and how You planned it that way. I guess I'm sleepy after all. **Good night**, God. I love You! Amen.

God, I Need to Talk to You about BEING A BAD SPORT

Written by Susan K. Leigh
Pictures by Bill Clark

CONCORDIA PUBLISHING HOUSE • SAINT LOUIS

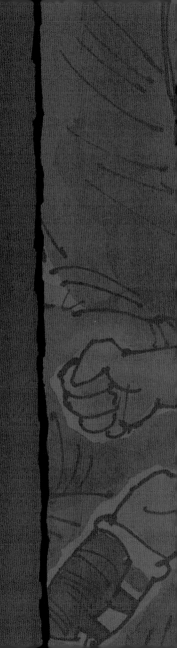

Sometimes I get tired of losing.
Sometimes I just want to win. Today, God,
I wanted to win the soccer game.
But we lost. **Again.**

It was the **last game.** The winners would have a pizza party and get trophies.

I was wide open, right in front of the net. Mike passed the ball to Taylor. Taylor kicked it and the goalie caught the ball. And we lost.

A hot-tempered one commits many sins. Proverbs 29:22

I was so angry I **shouted** at Taylor
and Mike. I was so disappointed I **wouldn't
shake hands** with the other players.
And I was so sad I **cried** on the way home.

Mom and Dad tried to make me feel better. "Do you want to go out for pizza?" Mom asked.

"No!" I said. "I'm not hungry! **I don't like pizza!**"

A fool gives full vent to his anger, but a wise man keeps himself under control. Proverbs 29:11

81

When we got home, Dad talked with me about winning and losing. He said that playing sports isn't only about learning to win and lose—it's about learning to be **part of a team** and **working together**.

"I know you wanted a trophy," Dad said. "But do you know what's better than a trophy? Do you know what **prize** you already have?"

I thought I knew, but I wasn't sure. "What prize?" I asked.

I press on toward the goal to win the prize for which God has called me heavenward in Christ Jesus. Philippians 3:14

Dad said nobody's perfect. Not Taylor
or Mike or me—or even the team that won
today. Only Jesus is perfect.

Jesus won the best prize of all—forgiveness. When Jesus died, He defeated sin, death,
and the devil. Because Jesus died for me,
I'm a winner too.

Once made perfect, He became the source of eternal salvation. Hebrews 5:9

So, God, now I understand about winning and losing. Even when I lose, I win the best prize ever—all because of what Jesus did for me. That's better than any old trophy! **Amen.**

God, I Need to Talk to You about BULLYING

Written by Susan K. Leigh
Pictures by Bill Clark

CONCORDIA PUBLISHING HOUSE • SAINT LOUIS

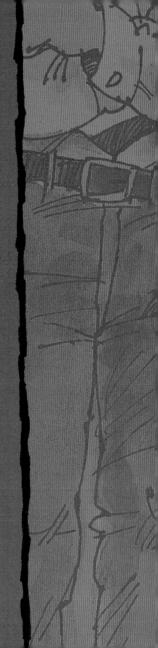

90

Dear God,

All I wanted was to be popular.
I wanted everyone to think I was cool.

Jason and Mike are the most popular boys in class and I wanted them to like me. Today they were mean to Samuel. So ... **I was mean to Samuel.**

Do not plot harm against your neighbor. Proverbs 3:29

First Jason and Mike teased Samuel.
Then they shoved him in the lunchroom.
I **laughed** at Samuel and **shoved** him too.
Samuel was brave and didn't say anything.
But I could tell he wanted to cry.

95

Mr. Miller saw the whole thing.
He called us, one by one, into the office to talk to us.

An evil man is snared by his own sin. Proverbs 29:6

I told him why I was mean to Samuel.
I said I was kind of afraid of Jason and Mike
but I wanted to be popular like they are.
I know that what I did was wrong. And
I feel really bad.

Mr. Miller said people did that to **Jesus.**
They made **fun of Him** and **hurt Him.**
They even **killed Him.** "You remember
what Jesus did on the cross, don't you?"
Mr. Miller asked. "He suffered and paid for
every one of their sins."

"Father, forgive them." Luke 23:34

I'm sorry I was mean to Samuel. I apologized to him and he forgave me. Samuel and I are friends now and I don't care anymore if Jason and Mike don't like me. Being popular doesn't matter to me either.

Those who plan what is good find love and faithfulness. Proverbs 14:22

What does matter, God, is that **You forgive me** all of my sins—even the big ones. You do this because Jesus died for my sins. **Thank You!** Amen.

God, I Need to Talk to You about CHEATING

Written by Dan Carr

Pictures by Bartholomew and Bill Clark

CONCORDIA PUBLISHING HOUSE • SAINT LOUIS

106

Dear God,

Yesterday my friends
got angry with me again.
They told me they will not play
with me anymore.

I love my friends
and I want to play with them.

You see, God, they caught me ...

cheating again.
The other day
I was playing checkers with Jack.
When he wasn't looking,
I moved one of his checkers.
When Jack saw what I had done,
he would not play with me anymore.

The riches you get by dishonesty soon disappear.
Proverbs 21:6 TEV

Another day I was playing tag
with Carlos, Jason, and Michael.
They are older and faster than I am.
   One time I almost tagged Carlos.
I yelled, **"Tagged you!"**
Everyone saw that I had missed.
So they would not let me play
with them anymore.

NOT FAIR NOT FAIR

Yesterday my brother and I were playing cards. I cheated again. He became very angry. So did I.

And I hit him with a block. He ran and told Mom.

I told Mom that my brother and my friends never let me win. **"It's not fair,"** I cried.

If you stir up anger,
you get into trouble.
Proverbs 30:33 TEV

Mom made me sit in a chair.
We had a long talk. She said,
"Nobody always wins.
We can only **do our best.**
When we cheat,
we never really learn how to win."

She handed me a puzzle
with all the pieces in place.
She said, "What fun would it be
if you **told** me you did the puzzle but
somebody else had?
When you cheat, you miss the real fun
of doing it yourself."

Mom also said,
"Cheating is like stealing.
You try to steal the 'win.'
But Jesus knows how much you
want to win. He forgives you and
wants to help you do your best."

Just as you received Christ Jesus
as Lord, continue to live in Him.
Colossians 2:6

Jesus,

I know that cheating is a sin.
Thank You for **forgiving** my sins.
Thank You also for Mom's talk.
Today I did not cheat,
and it was fun to play with my friends
and my brother.

Thank You, Jesus, for helping me
love others. Amen.

God, I Need to Talk to You about DISRESPECT

Written by Susan K. Leigh
Pictures by Bill Clark

CONCORDIA PUBLISHING HOUSE • SAINT LOUIS

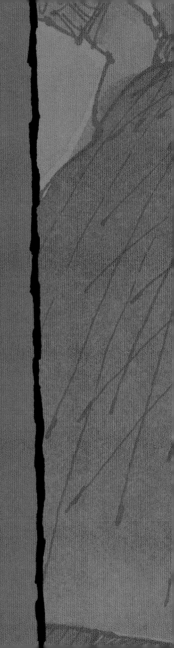

Dear God,

I have to stay in my room all afternoon and can't come out until it's time to eat. Mom told me to think about what I did and talk to You about it.

What I did was be mean. Mom said I was disrespectful. And, God, I was. I didn't even get caught for some of what I did. I'm really sorry about it.

Live in harmony with one another. Romans 12:16

Yesterday I ran into Jacob and he dropped everything. Jacob had to pick up all of his things and he was late for class.

It was my fault. And I didn't say I was sorry.

Today Sarah and Katie and I were playing jump rope. When Sarah missed, I giggled. Sarah said, "I'm not as good as you."

Then I said, **"Duh."** I could tell right away it made Sarah feel bad.

Katie said, "Let's go to my house to play."

In humility consider others better than yourselves. Philippians 2:3

Then I went inside. My brother was watching his favorite show. I didn't feel like watching it so I changed the channel. He yelled. I threw the remote on the floor.

Mom came into the room then and asked me to come talk with her.

He who loves a quarrel loves sin. Proverbs 17:19

Mom said, "Changing the channel when your brother was watching is wrong."

I said I knew that.

"And what you said to Sarah wasn't very nice." I said I knew that too. Then Mom said that You love everyone and provide for them.

Mom said we are to treat each other the same—loving, respectful, and forgiving—because that's how You treat us.

Mom said I need to apologize to my brother and Sarah. I will. And I'm going to apologize to Jacob, too, although she doesn't know about that.

Be imitators of God, therefore, as dearly loved children and live a life of love, just as Christ loved us. Ephesians 5:1–2

So now, God, I need Your forgiveness. I was rude and I am sorry. I need Your help too. Help me be nice to others and remember that we are all special in Your eyes. **Amen.**

God, I Need to Talk to You about FEELING SAD

Written by Susan K. Leigh
Pictures by Bill Clark

CONCORDIA PUBLISHING HOUSE · SAINT LOUIS

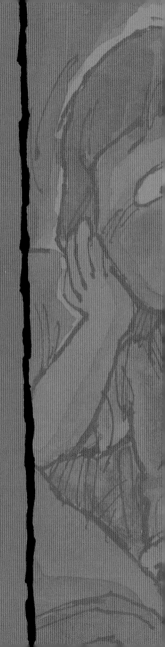

Dear Jesus,
I'm really sad. I feel like crying.

My dad said **it's okay** to feel sad. He said that everybody is sad sometimes.

141

He said that **sadness** comes
when we lose something or someone
we love. He told me he was sad when
his grandma died. (He said he cried
too.) And mom said she was sad when
her best friend moved away.

A time to weep, and a time to laugh.
Ecclesiastes 3:4

I understand that it's okay to be sad, Lord. But it's no fun. I don't want to be sad. I just want everything to be like it was before. I **just want to be happy** like I was before.

Mom told me that even You were sad. She said that when Your friend Lazarus died, **You cried**. That wasn't any fun for You, was it?

Jesus wept.
John 11:35

She said that in **heaven** there is no sadness. No one cries. I heard that in Sunday School too.

I know I won't feel like this forever. I know that You promise that one day everyone will be happy and there will be **no more crying**.

Joy comes in the morning.
Psalm 30:5

Thank You, Jesus!
Thank You for promising heaven to me. I feel better already. Amen!

God, I Need to Talk to You about GREED

Written by Susan K. Leigh
Pictures by Bill Clark

CONCORDIA PUBLISHING HOUSE · SAINT LOUIS

154

It all started when Joey and Jenny showed me their new trading cards yesterday.

Joey bought his with his saved-up allowance. Jenny bought hers with birthday money from her aunt. I already had a few cards, but I wanted new ones. **I wanted more** than Joey and Jenny had.

Give to everyone
who asks you. Luke 6:30

I remembered that I had some money
I'd been saving for the church missions project.
So I used all my money to buy trading cards.
Some were doubles. I was disappointed.
I didn't want more of the same cards.

Joey had a new one **I wanted,** but he wouldn't trade. Jenny didn't even let me see hers.

Sometimes it takes a painful experience to make us change our ways.
Proverbs 20:30 TEV

Then, in Sunday school this morning,
Mrs. Johnson asked for our offering for
the mission project. I didn't have anything
to give because I had spent my money on
trading cards.

Mrs. Johnson said, "That's okay. God will
use whatever we give."

But, God, I wanted to help other children learn about Jesus and how He died for their sins. All I have is trading cards that aren't worth anything. I don't even want to look at them today.

Dear God, I learned a valuable lesson. Being greedy is wrong. I learned that having more things isn't as important as **doing** more things—doing things that help others because we love You.

166

Be merciful just as your
Father is merciful. Luke 6:36

Dear Jesus,

You gave everything You had to pay for our sins. You gave Your life on the cross! I want to help others learn about Your love and forgiveness. So next time I have some money, I'm going to put it toward something that really counts! Amen.

God, I Need to Talk to You about HEALTHY EATING

Written by Susan K. Leigh

Pictures by Bill Clark

CONCORDIA PUBLISHING HOUSE • SAINT LOUIS

Hello, Lord,

You know everything about me. So that means You know I really like **candy**. And cookies. And chips.

And You know why I was **hungry** after school today. It's because at lunch I didn't eat my apple. I traded it for Blake's fruit gummies. I traded half of my turkey sandwich for Emma's potato chips. And I took a juice box and threw away my milk.

Do not desire his delicacies, for they are deceptive food.

Proverbs 23:3

My **stomach** hurt after lunch. I didn't feel like playing kick ball during recess. Instead I just sat on a swing until it was time to go in.

And I was **sleepy** during reading. Mrs. Wilke told me to sit up straight and pay attention.

Then she sent a **note** home for Mom.

All the toil of man is for his mouth, yet his appetite is not satisfied.

Ecclesiastes 7:3

Mom said the reason I was sleepy is because I had **too much** sugar at lunch. She said throwing away my milk and not eating all my sandwich is wasteful.

Dear God, I didn't mean to waste food. And really I didn't mean to give myself a **stomach ache**.

Then, at dinner, Mom and Dad explained about **healthy eating**.

Gracious words are like a honeycomb, sweetness to the soul and health to the body.

Proverbs 16:24

Dad said You made our bodies to work **best** when we eat healthy food. That means fruit, vegetables, milk, and meat. Dad said too much junk food hurts our bodies. When we hurt our bodies, we **dishonor** You, God—even if we don't mean to.

The heart of him who has understanding seeks knowledge, but the mouths of fools feed on folly.

Proverbs 15:14

So now I understand about healthy food. I want to honor You by taking care of myself. Tomorrow I'll eat the lunch Mom makes for me. And, God, thank You for giving me **good health**. In Jesus' name. Amen.

God, I Need to Talk to You about HOMEWORK

Written by Susan K. Leigh

Pictures by Bill Clark

CONCORDIA PUBLISHING HOUSE · SAINT LOUIS

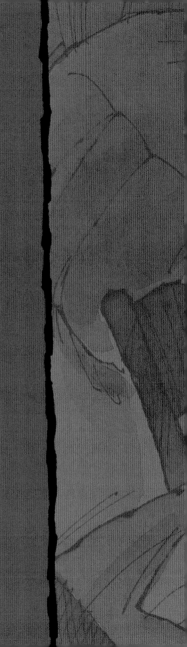

Dear God,
My favorite television show is on right now, and I can't watch it. That makes me really **unhappy**.

Mom said **I can't** watch television
until my homework is finished.

Wisdom will come into your heart, and knowledge will be pleasant to your soul.

Proverbs 2:10

My homework isn't finished because it's **boring**. Besides, I already learned all this stuff in school.

But Mom said that my teacher gives homework so I can practice what I learn. She said if I get my homework wrong, it means I need more practice or extra help. If I get it right, it means I **learned it well**.

The sluggard is wiser in his own eyes than seven men who can answer sensibly.

Proverbs 26:16

And Mom said that everybody has a job to do and **my job** is to go to school and do my homework. I also have to take out the trash and feed the dog and make my bed. Doing my job makes **You** happy.

She also said that my homework wouldn't take so long if I would just concentrate.

So I stopped complaining and did what Mom said.

She was right! I finished all my homework in a few minutes. It wasn't as boring as it thought it would be. (It was actually kind of fun!)

He who walks in wisdom will be delivered.
Proverbs 28:26

I feel a lot better because it's done and I'm ready to learn new things tomorrow. In fact, I think I might be a little **smarter** already!

Now, I can watch the rest of my favorite television show.

Give her of the fruit of her hands, and let
her works praise her in the gates.

Proverbs 31:31

I never thought I would say this, but thank You, God, for **homework**. I like to learn, and I love to please You. In Jesus' name. Amen!

God, I Need to Talk to You about HURTING OTHERS

Written by Dan Carr

Pictures by Bartholomew and Bill Clark

CONCORDIA PUBLISHING HOUSE • SAINT LOUIS

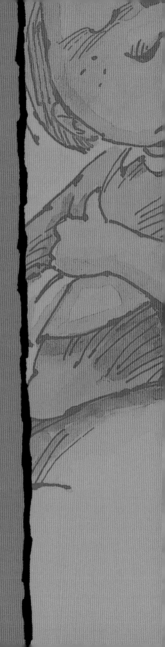

202

CRY CRY

CRY

Dear God,
My baby sister spilt her milk
on my coloring book.
It was a mess.
I was so angry
I shoved her.
She cried.

203

At school today, two boys were **yelling** at each other. Then they **hit** each other. A teacher made them stop.

Blessed are the peacemakers,
for they will be called
sons of God.

Matthew 5:9

Madison came to school
today with a **black eye.** She said,
"My brother was angry with me and hit me."

Mom and Dad were talking at supper tonight. Dad said, "The news report said a man was in the hospital. Someone was **angry and hurt him.**"

You shall not murder.
Exodus 20:13

Mom and Dad love me,
but they feel sad when I get angry
and do bad things. They tell me,
"It is wrong to hurt others."
Sometimes they **punish me,**
but not too much.
I know they really love me.

God, it **scares me** when
I see others get hurt because
someone was angry.

I think about that when I get angry
with my sister.

I also think about how
people hurt Your Son, Jesus,
even when He loved them.
I want to be like Jesus.

Love each other as I have loved you.
John 15:12

Dear Jesus,
When I get angry,
I forget about Your love.
Help me remember that You died
on the cross to **forgive me**
and to give me Your love.
When I want to hurt others, help me
show Your **love** instead. Thank You, Jesus.
Amen.

God, I Need to Talk to You about LAZINESS

Written by Susan K. Leigh

Pictures by Bill Clark

CONCORDIA PUBLISHING HOUSE • SAINT LOUIS

218

Dear God, here's how this whole thing started. Mom told me it was my turn to help in the kitchen. I said I would do it later. Right then I wanted to watch television.

Then she said to clean my room.
I started to, but I stopped to play a game.
I played for an hour.

When Mom saw me, she wasn't happy.
Mom took the game. "You'll get it back
when your room is clean," she said.

Children, obey your parents in everything, for this pleases the Lord. Colossians 3:20

It didn't take long to clean my room. Mom gave me back the game.

Then my sister asked me to help her practice free throws because her team has a tournament next week. I like basketball. I like my sister. But I wanted to play my game again. So I did.

That's when Mom took the game again and said to **stop being so lazy** and get some exercise.

"It's not good for you," she told me. "You can have this game back in one week."

Lazy hands make a man poor.
Proverbs 10:4

"It's okay to play computer games sometimes. But it's also important to get your work done and to be helpful to others. When you do what is expected of you, you **serve** God."

I had never thought of it that way.

Mom said, "God has important work for each of us." Her job is to be my mom and take care of me. That includes teaching me what I need to know—like how to be responsible and not waste time.

Mom said my important work is to be a son and brother.

In Christ we who are many form one body, and each member belongs to all the others. Romans 12:5

Mom said, "When we do our job, we glorify God."

Now that she put it that way, Lord, I want to be the best I can be so I can serve and honor You.

Helping people and getting my work done feels **good**.

Whatever you do, work at it with all your heart, as working for the Lord.
Colossians 3:23

But more than that, I want to glorify You because You have already done so much for me, like sending me a Savior— Jesus—who died for my sins. **Thanks, God! Amen.**

God, I Need to Talk to You about LYING

Written by Dan Carr

Pictures by Bartholomew and Bill Clark

CONCORDIA PUBLISHING HOUSE • SAINT LOUIS

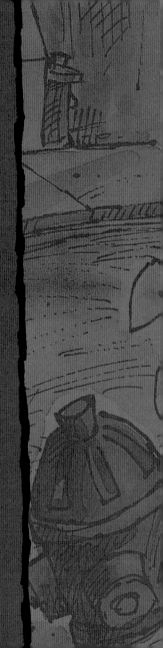

234

Dear God,

I feel bad inside.
I did something wrong
and I need to talk with You.
When I did it, I hurt You and
Mom and a nice man.
What I did today was ...

I told a lie.

I was walking home from school
and walked through Mr. Green's
pretty flowers.

I did not look where I was going.
I tripped and fell on the flowers.
Boy! Did I make a mess!

TRiP

When I did not confess my sins,
I was worn out from crying all day long.

Psalm 32:3

237

I ran home. I was scared.
Mom asked, "Why are you so dirty?"
I said, "I fell at school."
Then I went to my bedroom.
After a little while,
Mom called me to the kitchen
and told me to sit on a chair.

UM. WELL

Mom said, "Mr. Green phoned. He saw you fall and run away. He was afraid you were hurt. I am glad you are all right, but **why did you lie** to me?"

A lie has a short life,
but the truth lives on forever.
Proverbs 12:19

"When you lie," Mom said, "you hurt the person you lie to, and **you hurt God** because He loves you."

Mom told me that to feel better inside I had to do two things.

First, I had to tell You and Mom
that I was sorry.

I already told Mom.
Now I am telling You.

Mom says that if I ask You,
You will **forgive me** because
Jesus died for my sins.

Dear Jesus,

Sometimes I am afraid
to tell the truth.

Forgive me, Jesus,
and help me be brave enough
to always tell the truth.

Happy are those whose sins are forgiven.
Psalm 31:1

Now, God, I have to say Amen. I want and need to tell Mr. Green that I am sorry. When I ran away, I lied to him too. **I am sorry.** I love You, Jesus. Amen.

God, I Need to Talk to You about MY PARENTS

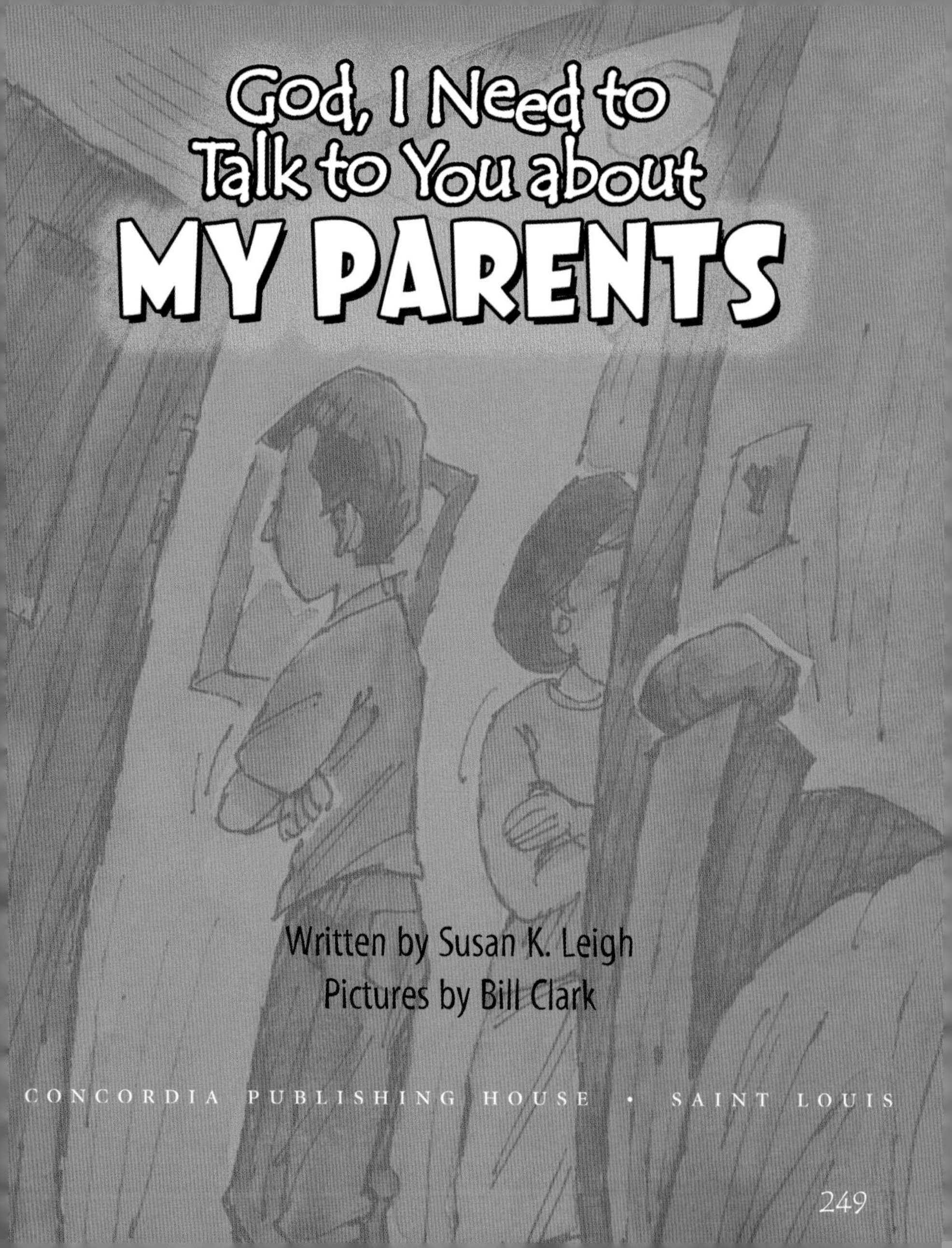

Written by Susan K. Leigh

Pictures by Bill Clark

CONCORDIA PUBLISHING HOUSE • SAINT LOUIS

GULP!

Dear God,
My mom and dad had
a **fight** today.

I think they were **trying to be quiet** about it, but I heard them anyway.

Anxiety in a man's heart
weighs him down.
Proverbs 12:25

It makes me scared when they fight. Taylor's mom and dad used to have fights and now they don't live together anymore. **I'm afraid** that will happen to us too.

When I am afraid, I put my trust in You.

Psalm 56:3

I asked Mom **if everything was okay** and she said yes, but I could tell that she had been crying. Dad was real quiet, but he gave me a hug and then he played checkers with me.

After supper, Mom asked
if I was okay.

She said that she was sorry
and she knew that things were
hard for me. She said things were
hard for all of us right now.

I asked her what was going to happen to us. She said she didn't know, but she said there was one thing she did know—that she and Dad **love me very much**.

She said that You and Jesus
love me very much too. And then
mom said a **prayer** with me. That
made both of us feel better.
(Remember, God? That's when I
asked You to help them not fight.)

Out of my distress I called on the Lord.

Psalm 118:5

I know that whatever happens,
Lord, You will **always** be with me.
Thank You. And thank You for loving
me and my mom and dad too. Amen.

God, I Need to Talk to You about
PAYING ATTENTION

Written by Dan Carr

Pictures by Bartholomew and Bill Clark

CONCORDIA PUBLISHING HOUSE · SAINT LOUIS

Dear God,

Once again I missed out
on a lot of fun today.
I know the reason why, and it is my fault.
I have trouble ...

paying attention.

This morning
I was supposed to go with my friend Rick
and his mother to play ball, have a picnic,
and then go roller-skating.

Ears that hear and eyes that see—
the LORD has made them both.

Proverbs 20:12

I told Mom I was supposed to be at Rick's house at 10 o'clock.
We went shopping first and got to Rick's house 10 minutes early.
There was **no one there.**
They had already left. Without me.
I was so hurt I cried.

271

After supper, Rick's mom
telephoned and asked Mom
why I was not there at 9 o'clock.
"I told Jimmy three times that
we were leaving at **9 o'clock,**" she said.
Mom said, "He has a problem.
Jimmy worries so much about himself
that he doesn't always pay attention."

Cast all your anxiety on Him because He cares for you.
1 Peter 5:7

God, Mom is right.
I do worry so much about **myself**
that I do not pay attention to others.
I even get poor grades in school
because I do not listen.

God, I miss out on a lot of things. Sometimes things **go wrong** because I do not pay attention. Mom says that You gave me ears for a reason.

Dear Jesus,
Help me use the ears You gave me.
Forgive me when I think only
about myself and do not care about
others or pay attention to them.

Cast your cares on the LORD
and He will sustain you.
Psalm 55:22

I am thankful that **You pay attention** to me and that You are not too busy to hear me. Thank You for loving me and for forgiving my sins. You really do care about me. And thank You for my ears. Amen.

Me Too

God, I Need to Talk to You about SCHOOL

Written by Susan K. Leigh
Pictures by Bill Clark

CONCORDIA PUBLISHING HOUSE • SAINT LOUIS

281

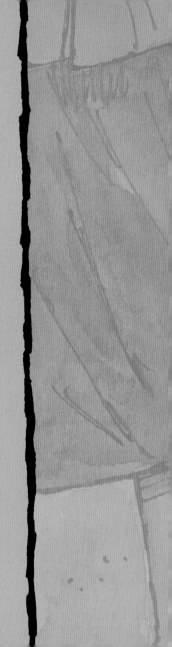

Dear God,
I don't like **school**.
And I don't want to
go any more.

I don't want to go because
I'm **not very good** at school.
Other kids are better. Sometimes
I just don't understand things.

Apply your heart to instruction and your ear to words of knowledge.

Proverbs 23:12

Mom said that everybody has to go to school. She said there's no other way. She asked me what the **problem** was.

287

I told her that Kaitlyn made fun of me because I didn't know the math answers and she did. That's why **I don't want to go** to school anymore.

I told her that Mrs. Cooper **helps me** at recess. I don't want to stay in at recess. I want to go outside to play with my friends.

Mom said she was sorry about Kaitlyn. She said it was good that Mrs. Cooper was helping me and she and Dad would help me too. And she said she was certain that I would catch on.

That made me feel **better**.

Know that wisdom is such to your soul; if you find it, there will be a future.

Proverbs 24:14

293

Mom said **I can pray to You** anytime I feel upset about school. She said that would help me feel better so I can focus on learning.

I know that will work because You always hear our prayers in Jesus' name. So, Lord, would You help me enjoy school more? Would You help me learn?

I guess **I'll try school again**. I'll listen closely and pay attention. I won't let Kaitlyn bother me. I'll pray to You when I feel upset. And I'll remember that Jesus loves me and forgives me. Thank You, God. Thank You for hearing me! Amen.

God, I Need to Talk to You about
SHARING

Written by Dan Carr

Pictures by Bartholomew and Bill Clark

CONCORDIA PUBLISHING HOUSE • SAINT LOUIS

298

Dear God,

Today, I had a bag of candy and I ate it all myself. I would not give any to my sister or my little brother or to my parents.

Yesterday, I had a bag of popcorn at the movies and **I did not share** any with my friends.

Give to everyone who asks you. Luke 6:30

Today, God, I learned a lesson.
My friends were playing ball.
I wanted to play too, **but**
they would not share the ball.

I went home.

My brother and sister and parents
were eating a big bowl of popcorn.
They would not share it.

Sometimes it takes a painful experience
to make us change our ways.

Proverbs 20:30 TEV

I felt lonely.
I felt angry.
I sat on my back stairs.

My family came outside.
Then my friends came around
the side of the house.

They told me they felt hurt
when I would not share.

They told me You said,
"It is more blessed to give
than to receive" (Acts 20:35).

309

Then they did a **special** thing.
My brother and sister **gave me**
a bag of popcorn they had saved.
Then I played ball with my friends.
I was really happy!
It **IS** more fun to share.

Be merciful just as your Father is merciful.
Luke 6:36

Dear Jesus,

You gave me so much love when You died for my sins. And I know You shared with me all the things that I have. I know it is wrong when I don't share. Forgive me.

Help me share my things and especially share Your love. Amen.

God, I Need to Talk to You about STEALING

Written by Dan Carr

Pictures by Bartholomew and Bill Clark

CONCORDIA PUBLISHING HOUSE · SAINT LOUIS

313

314

Dear God,

You promised that when I hurt inside I can talk to You.

I know You love me. Well, I did something wrong today. I am sorry. Today ...

I stole a candy bar.

I was shopping with my mother.
We were in the line
where we pay for things.
I picked up a candy bar
and put it in my pocket.

You shall not steal.

Exodus 20:15

I know I was wrong.
My Sunday school teacher
told me what You said.
You said **it is wrong** to steal.
My mom says so too.

319

In the store I asked Mom
to buy the candy. She said no.
But it looked **so good!**
So I took it anyway.
I knew it was wrong.

If we have food and clothes,
that should be enough for us.

1 Timothy 6:8 TEV

Then a bad thing happened
to me that was good. My mom saw me.
She was **upset** with me.
She made me put the candy back.
Then I had to tell the store lady
what I did and that I was sorry.
That was not easy.

323

Before Mom punished me at home, she explained that the candy **belonged** to the store. When I took it without paying for it, I was stealing.

Then Mom told me that
Your Son, Jesus, loves me.
When He died on the cross,
He paid for my sins (like stealing).
She said I should talk to You
and tell You what I did
and that I am sorry.
Jesus, I really am sorry.

If we confess our sins, He will . . .
forgive us our sins. 1 John 1:9

327

Dear Jesus,

I was wrong when I took something that was not mine. I know I hurt others when I steal. Please, forgive me.

Thank You for dying for my sins. Help my life show that I love You. Amen.

God, I Need to Talk to You about
TALKING BACK

Written by Susan K. Leigh
Pictures by Bill Clark

CONCORDIA PUBLISHING HOUSE • SAINT LOUIS

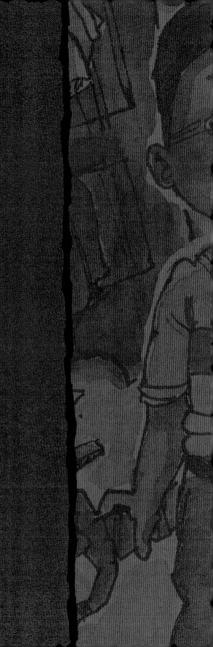

Dear Jesus,

I don't know why I said it.
It just came out.

Mom told me to put my things
away and wash up for dinner. I wanted to
keep playing so **I ignored her**. She told
me again. And I ignored her again.

A wise son hears his
father's instruction.
Proverbs 13:1

When she said it the third time, she was angry. I rolled my eyes. I made a face. And I said, "**I will!** You don't have to yell!" My mom was really unhappy about that.

335

So here I am—**in trouble** again.
No toys. No television. And no
talking back.

No ill befalls the righteous, but the wicked are filled with trouble.   Proverbs 12:21

I didn't mean to **talk back**.
I was sorry as soon as I said it.

Dad said that Mom had already told me twice to get ready for dinner. He said she shouldn't have to tell me **three times**.

I told them I was sorry.

Mom reminded me about the **Ten Commandments**. She talked about the "honor your parents" one and said that means I'm supposed to watch what I say. Then mom said that when I mess up, You forgive me. She said she forgives me too. She said forgiveness is what being baptized is about.

Honor your father and your mother.

Deuteronomy 5:16

I know that my mom is right.
I feel really bad that I yelled at her.
I won't do it anymore. And **I'll try really hard** to do what she says the first time she says it.

Lord, I'm happy that **Mom forgives me**. She's the best! And Jesus, thank You for forgiving me too. **Amen!**

God, I Need to Talk to You about VANDALISM

Written by Dan Carr

Pictures by Bartholomew and Bill Clark

CONCORDIA PUBLISHING HOUSE · SAINT LOUIS

346

Dear God,

It seemed to be a good idea at the time. But our school principal, Mr. Johnson, called it ...

vandalism.

    It all happened because of Jack.
Yesterday, he ran his blue bike
into my friend, Sam (Samantha).
    So today, Sam brought
a can of green spray paint
to school and we "painted" Jack's bike.

Love your enemies
and pray for those who persecute you.
Matthew 5:44

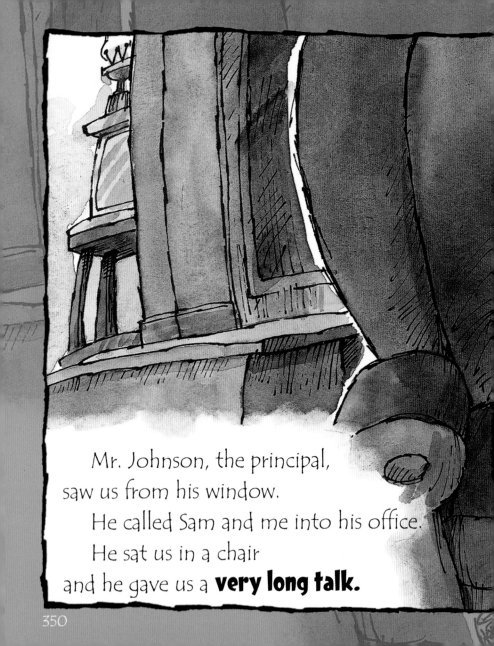

Mr. Johnson, the principal,
saw us from his window.
　　He called Sam and me into his office.
　　He sat us in a chair
and he gave us a **very long talk.**

He said,
"You did a very **bad thing.**
It's called vandalism"
   "Jack is a bully.
He deserved it," we replied.
   "Even if Jack is a bully,"
Mr. Johnson said, "you were
wrong to damage his bike."

Do not repay anyone evil for evil ...
but overcome evil with good.

Romans 12:17, 21

When I got home,
Mom and Dad punished me.
They also told me that
You are not happy when
I hurt others or their things.
Dear Jesus, forgive me.

When I saw Jack this afternoon,
I told him I was sorry.
   Sam said so too.
   Then we helped him
repaint his bike.
   And, You know what, God?
Jack forgave us—just as You do!

Now we're **friends.**
Jack and Sam and I played and
shared with one another today.
And Jack stopped being a bully.

Forgive one another,
as God has forgiven
you through Christ.

Ephesians 4:32 TEV

Jesus,

Forgive me for hurting Jack. I know damaging other people's things is always wrong. Thank You for loving me even when I am bad. Help me to love others, even when they mistreat me. Amen.

God, I Need to Talk to You about VIDEO GAMES

Written by Susan K. Leigh
Pictures by Bill Clark

CONCORDIA PUBLISHING HOUSE · SAINT LOUIS

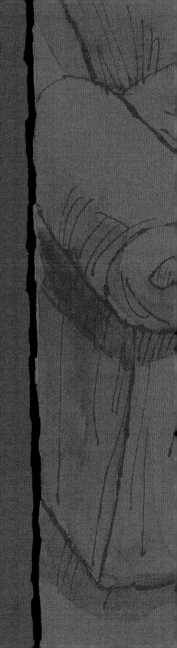

Dear Jesus,

I **love** playing video games.

I'd rather play video games than do anything else. Especially homework or chores.

It's even **more fun** when my friends come over to play video games with me.

But Mom and Dad say I can't play video games **all the time**. They say I need to do other things too, like read a book or go outdoors to play.

I like to do those things. But I like video games more.

The way of a sluggard is like a hedge of thorns, but the path of the upright is a level highway.

Proverbs 15:19

Mom said that today I overdid it with video games. She said it's not healthy to sit indoors all the time, and I need to get some **exercise**.

I told Mom I get exercise playing video games.

Mom told me she didn't like my attitude. So now I'm **grounded** from all my video games for two whole weeks.

By insolence comes nothing but strife, but
with those who take advice is wisdom.

Proverbs 13:10

Mom said that when I get them back, I have to choose between thirty minutes of video games and thirty minutes of television.

That's a **really hard** choice.

Good sense is a fountain of life to him who
has it, but the instruction of fools is folly.
Proverbs 16:22

Dad said maybe I could take turns—television one day and video games the next.
I think that's a **good idea**.

Good sense wins favor.
Proverbs 13:15

And you know what, Lord? Playing outdoors is lot of **fun**. I guess giving up video games for a while won't be so bad after all! Amen. (P.S. I asked Mom to forgive me for being rude.)

God, I Need to Talk to You about

WHINING

Written by Susan K. Leigh
Pictures by Bill Clark

CONCORDIA PUBLISHING HOUSE · SAINT LOUIS

378

Hello God,

My dad says I need to talk to You. He says I have a habit that needs to be broken and You'll help me break it.

Dad says **I whine too much.** He says that whining annoys people and is disrespectful. That's why I keep getting in trouble for doing it.

Last week, I lost an hour of television time because **I whined about having to do my homework.** I didn't want to practice my spelling words. I wanted to watch my favorite cartoon instead.

A fool's mouth is his undoing. Proverbs 18:7

Yesterday, I wanted to go to the park with my brother. But I couldn't ride my bike because I was grounded for whining about having to make my bed. I stayed home by myself—and **I whined about it.**

Today, I was hungry and wanted a snack. Mom said dinner was in an hour and a snack would spoil my appetite. Dad heard me whine about it. Now I have to sit here and think about **how to break my bad habit.**

I don't mean to whine. But I want people to **listen to me** or to **help me right away.** Sometimes they're busy and I don't want to wait. Sometimes I feel like I'm not very important.

The quiet words of the wise are more to be heeded. Ecclesiastes 9:17

Dad says whining doesn't show your love to other people. I think Dad's right— **whining is wrong.** I want to be nice to others because Jesus loves me and died for my sins. Besides, I don't like it when other people whine.

I am sorry I was annoying. I want to break my bad habit. So, Lord, I need Your help. Forgive me and help me learn to be patient and to show respect—for Jesus' sake. Thanks, God. Amen.